The Robotx
Get Help from Simple Machines

Pressing Down

The Lever

Written by Gerry Bailey

Illustrated by Mike Spoor

The Robotx
Get Help from Simple Machines

Crabtree Publishing Company
www.crabtreebooks.com
1-800-387-7650

PMB 59051, 350 Fifth Ave.
59ₜₕ Floor,
New York, NY 10118

616 Welland Ave.
St. Catharines, ON
L2M 5V6

Published by Crabtree Publishing in 2014

Author: Gerry Bailey
Illustrator: Mike Spoor
Editor: Kathy Middleton
Proofreader: Crystal Sikkens
End matter: Kylie Korneluk
Production coordinator and
   Prepress technician: Ken Wright
Print coordinator: Margaret Amy Salter

Copyright © 2013
BrambleKids Ltd.

Photographs:
All images are Shutterstock.com unless otherwise stated.
Pg 17 G10ck
Pg 19 – ER_09
Pg 24 – El Greco
Pg 25 – (t) Christopher Elwell (b) Jake Rennaker

Printed in Canada/022014/MA20131220

Library and Archives Canada Cataloguing in Publication

Bailey, Gerry, author
     Pressing down : the lever / written by Gerry Bailey ; illustrated by Mike Spoor.

(The robotx get help from simple machines)
Includes index.
Issued in print and electronic formats.
ISBN 978-0-7787-0416-4 (bound).--ISBN 978-0-7787-0422-5 (pbk.).--
ISBN 978-1-4271-7534-2 (pdf).--ISBN 978-1-4271-7528-1 (html)

     1. Levers--Juvenile literature. I. Spoor, Mike, illustrator II. Title.

TJ147.B34 2014   j621.8   C2013-908709-5
                                        C2013-908710-9

Library of Congress Cataloging-in-Publication Data

Bailey, Gerry, author.
 Pressing down : the lever / written by Gerry Bailey ; illustrated by Mike Spoor.
     pages cm. -- (The Robotx get help from simple machines)
 Audience: Ages 5-8.
 Audience: K to grade 3.
 Includes index.
 ISBN 978-0-7787-0416-4 (reinforced library binding) -- ISBN 978-0-7787-0422-5 (pbk.) -- ISBN 978-1-4271-7534-2 (electronic pdf) -- ISBN 978-1-4271-7528-1 (electronic html)
1. Levers--Juvenile literature. 2. Simple machines--Juvenile literature. I. Spoor, Mike, illustrator. II. Title. III. Title: Lever.

TJ147.B245 2014
621.8'11--dc23
                                        2013050841

Contents

The
Robotx

Meet   and

RobbO   RobbEE

The robots' workshop

RobbO and RobbEE are usually very, very busy in their workshop...

making all kinds of useful (and not so useful) machines.

Machines like this...

and this.

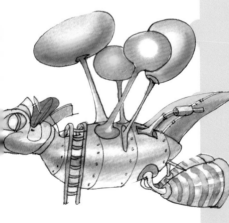

A machine is...

A machine is a tool used to make work easier. Work is the effort needed to create force. A force is a push or pull on an object. Machines allow us to push, pull, or lift a heavy weight much easier, or using less effort. All machines are made up of at least one **simple machine**.

There are six kinds of simple machines. Some have just one part that moves. Others are made up of two or more parts. The six simple machines are:

- **lever**
- **wedge**
- **pulley**
- **screw**
- **inclined plane**
- **wheel and axle**

This book is about the lever.

The two robots are painting the walls of their workshop.

RobbO can't reach the low parts because he's high up on the ladder.

RobbEE can't reach the high parts because he's down on the ground.

There's no way they can each paint both the high parts and the low parts working this way.

Or is there?

RobbO has an idea! He finds a long board and a large round can. Together they roll the can under the board so it is evenly balanced.

"We have made a lever," says RobbO, "and we'll use it like a seesaw."

But the lever won't rock up and down unless there is a heavy and a light end. The heavy end will always be down. The light end will always be up.

"You take the paint can," says Robb0. "I'll paint up high, and you paint down low."

"Now, pass me the paint can," says RobbO, "and the seesaw will tilt the other way."

Lever words

The lever is one of the oldest tools ever used by people to help them do work.

A lever has a bar, or arm, that rests on something called a fulcrum. The fulcrum can be placed anywhere under the arm.

You can push up or pull down one end of the arm to make the other end move. The pushing or pulling is called the effort.

The object being moved is called the load.

There are different kinds of levers, but they all use effort, a fulcrum, an arm, and a load.

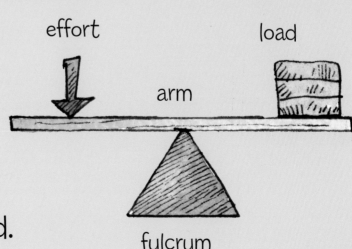

effort

load

arm

fulcrum

Archimedes' claw

Over lunch, RobbO tells the story of Archimedes' claw.

Archimedes was a **mathematician** and **inventor** who lived more than 2,000 years ago in the city of Syracuse, which was then part of Greece. During a war with the Romans, a huge fleet of ships came to attack their city.

Archimedes was asked to invent a machine that could defend the city walls along the sea. His brilliant invention used a kind of lever. His workmen built a long wooden arm that rested on the seawall. The wall was used as a fulcrum. The longer part of the arm was on the city's side of the wall. The shorter part was over the sea.

Attached to the end of the shorter arm was a rope with a device that had many hooks like a claw. On the city's side, the Greek defenders could move the arm up and down.

When the Roman ships arrived, the Greeks went to work. They locked the hooks onto a Roman ship's sides, then pulled the lever down so the ship was pulled up and tipped over. Syracuse was saved, thanks to Archimedes' claw.

The paint can needs to be put away on a high shelf.

RobbO moves the lever's arm a bit so the fulcrum is not in the middle. One side of the board is shorter now. He puts the load on the shorter end.

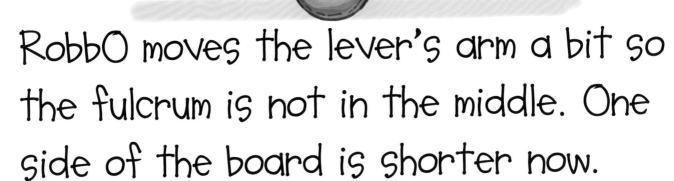

They push the longer side down, but they can't raise the can all the way up.

So RobbO makes the longer side even longer. Will this do the trick? No!

Finally RobbO shifts the arm to make the long side much, much longer. Now they both push down—and the load goes up.

"Awesome!" they cheer.

A very tall lever

A crane is a special kind of lever. It is made up of a beam, or arm, attached to a fulcrum. One end of the beam is shorter than the other. The longer arm is the lifting arm. **Concrete** slabs called counterweights are attached to the shorter end of the beam to help balance the crane when it is lifting a heavy load.

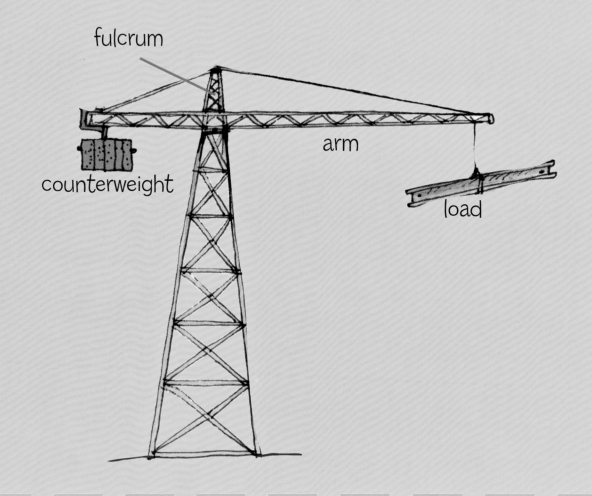

fulcrum

arm

counterweight

load

Tower cranes are often used in the construction of tall buildings.

Picking up the paint

RobbO has gone to get more paint. He has taken the wheelbarrow because the cans are heavy.

"It will be a lot easier with a wheelbarrow," says RobbO.

The wheelbarrow is a lever, too, but it is different from the seesaw board. Its load is placed in the middle.

load

effort

fulcrum

Fishing with a lever

The Robotx have been busy all day using their levers in the workshop to help lift loads. Now they use levers in the park to help them catch fish!

Your arm is a lever. The effort is the muscle in your arm, the fulcrum is your elbow, and your hand holds the load.

A fishing rod is also a lever, but it's different from the seesaw and the wheelbarrow. The fish is the load, and the effort is the fisherman's hand. The handle of the pole is the fulcrum.

Three kinds of lever

A first-class lever has the fulcrum between the effort and the load.

A seesaw is a good example of a first-class lever.

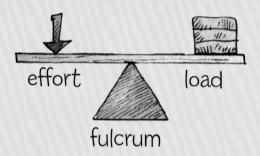

effort   load

fulcrum

A second-class lever has the fulcrum at one end, the effort at the other end, and the load in the middle.

A wheelbarrow is a second-class lever.

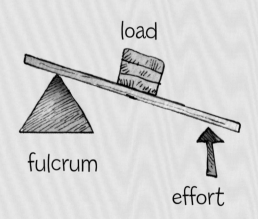

load

fulcrum

effort

A third-class lever has the fulcrum at one end, the effort in the middle, and the load at the other end.

A fishing rod is a good example of a third-class lever.

effort

fulcrum

load

Lots of levers

Levers are used in many different ways. Sometimes they are used with other simple machines.

Nutcracker

A nutcracker is a lever with the load in the middle. The fulcrum is at the joined end. The effort is created by pushing the handles together.

Can opener

The handles of a can opener act as a lever. The lever is used to press a wheel-shaped blade into the top of a can.

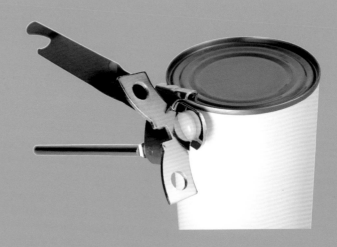

Seesaw

A seesaw is a first-class lever with the fulcrum in the middle of the arm. The riders at each end take turns being the load and the effort.

A claw hammer

The head, or top, of the hammer acts as the fulcrum. The load is the nail that the claw grips. At the other end, the effort is made by pulling down on the handle of the hammer.

Digger

A digger is a large machine used to remove earth and stones from the ground. It is used to build roads and dig out tunnels.

The digger moves around on steel **treads** linked together, called a caterpillar track.

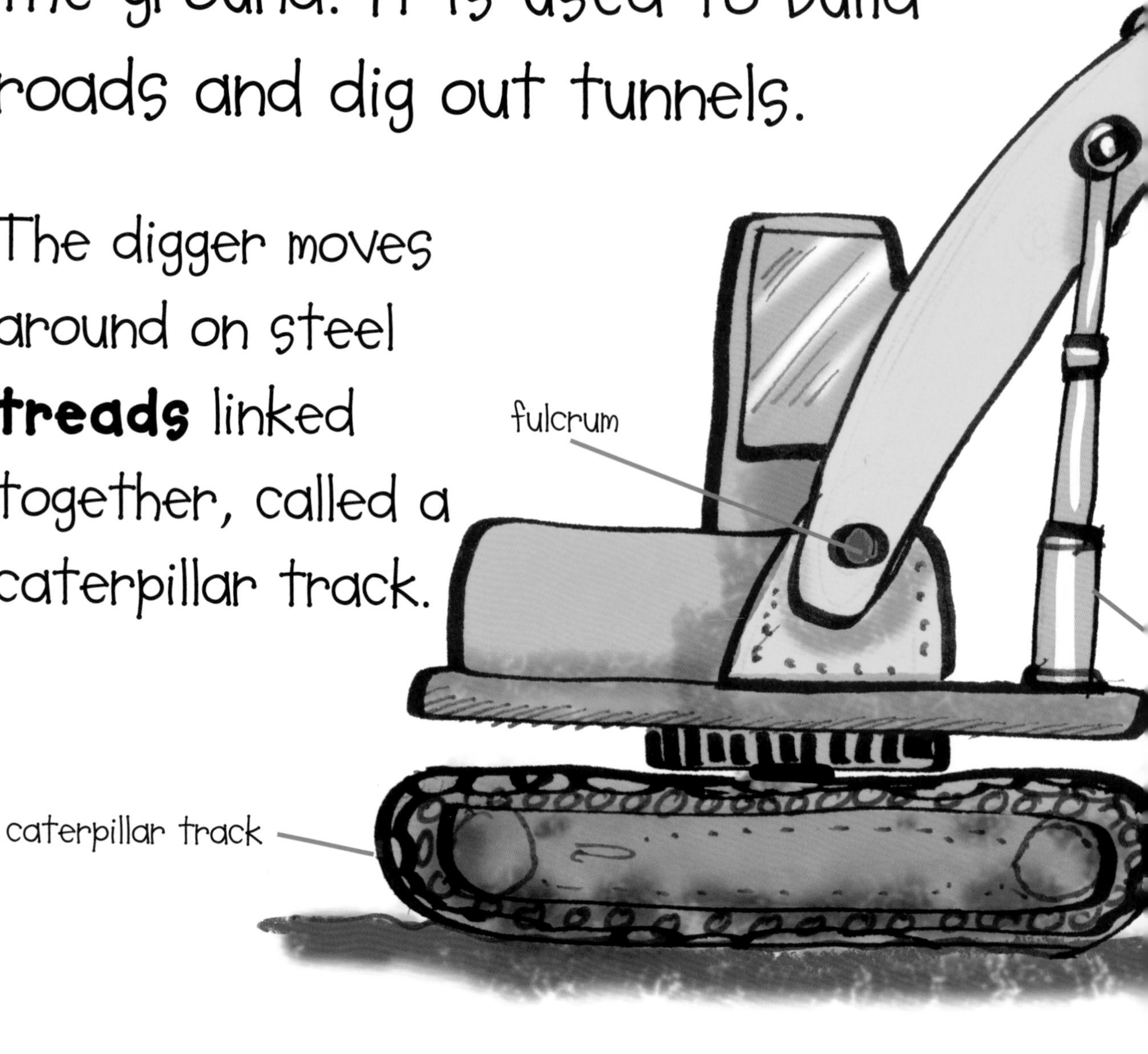

fulcrum

caterpillar track

The effort is supplied by the **hydraulic cylinder** in the middle. Hydraulic machines create power using fluid such as oil.

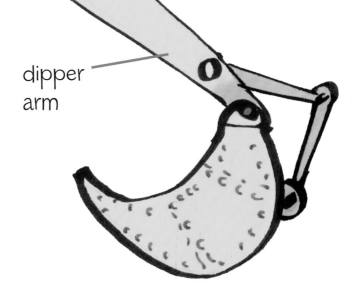

boom

The main arm of a digger is called a boom. This arm is the kind of lever where the effort is in the middle.

dipper arm

hydraulic cylinder

The load is in the bucket attached to the dipper arm.

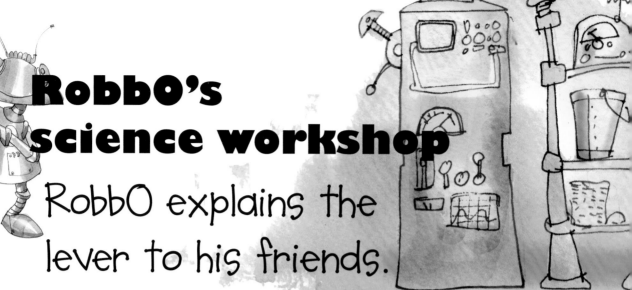

Robbo's science workshop

RobbO explains the lever to his friends.

A lever is a simple machine that looks like a bar or board. The bar, called the arm, balances on a fulcrum. A lever is used to lift loads or to move them.

effort

load

fulcrum

You use force, called the effort, at one end of the arm. This lifts the load at the other end of the arm.

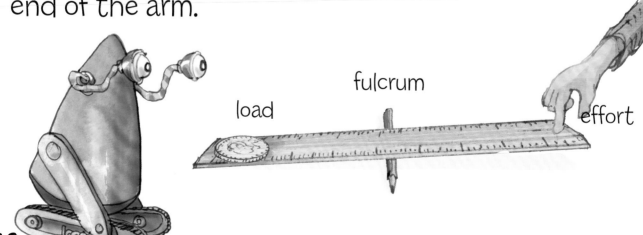

load

fulcrum

effort

If you increase the distance between the effort and the fulcrum, the effort needed to lift the load is less. This way you can lift a bigger load. However, the distance you can raise it is less.

load

effort

fulcrum

29

Build a catapult

The Robotx think of another clever use for a lever. They build one that will help them score at basketball!

This kind of catapult is known as a trebuchet. It was used hundreds of years ago to fire objects at the castle walls of enemies.

When RobbO drops a heavy frog robot onto the short end of the arm below, it will create a force that will tilt the long end of the arm upward. The ball at the end of the long arm will shoot into the air toward the net.

Learning more

Books

Get to Know: Levers
By Karen Volpe
(Crabtree Publishing, 2009)

How Toys Work: Levers
By Sian Smith
(Heinemann, 2012)

Levers
By David Armentrout and Patricia Armentrout
(Rourke Publishing, 2009)

Websites

www.ducksters.com/science/simple_machines.php
A simple description on what a lever is and what it is used for.

www.mocomi.com/lever/
An animated video and summary of the workings of a lever.

www.bbc.co.uk/learningzone/clips/how-do-levers-work/6660.html
A clip investigating how levers work.

Glossary

concrete A hard, strong building material made of sand, gravel, pebbles, broken stone, or cement

hydraulic cylinder A machine powered by fluid

inclined plane A slanted surface connecting a lower point to a higher point

invention Something that has been created

inventor A person who creates things

lever A bar that rests on a support called a fulcrum which lifts or moves loads

mathematician A person who is very good at math

pulley A simple machine that uses grooved wheels and a rope to raise, lower, or move a load

screw An inclined plane wrapped around a pole which holds things together or lifts materials

simple machine A machine that makes work easier by transferring force from one point to another

treads The rubber on a tire or track that helps grip a surface

wedge Two inclined planes joined together used to split things

wheel and axle A wheel with a rod, called an axle, through its center which lifts or moves load

Index